Working Together Against
TEEN SUICIDE

Suicides are tragedies. Teens can become involved in suicide prevention programs to reach out to other teens in need.

❖ THE LIBRARY OF SOCIAL ACTIVISM ❖

Working Together Against
TEEN SUICIDE

Toby Axelrod

THE ROSEN PUBLISHING GROUP, INC.
NEW YORK

Published in 1996 by The Rosen Publishing Group, Inc.
29 East 21st Street, New York, NY 10010

First Edition

Library of Congress Cataloging-in-Publication Data

Axelrod, Toby.
    Working together against teen suicide / by Toby Axelrod.
       p.   cm. — (The Library of social activism)
    Includes bibliographical references and index.
    Summary: Explains why some teenagers consider suicide and presents several ways young people might help prevent this course of action, including peer counseling, staffing telephone hotlines, and using cyberspace to connect with suicidal teenagers.
    ISBN 0-8239-2261-8
    1. Teenagers—Suicidal behavior—United States—Juvenile literature. [1. Suicide]. I. Title. II. Series.
HV6546.A84   1996
362.2′87′0835—dc20   96-6960
                                        CIP
                                        AC

Contents

INTRODUCTION

WHY DO SOME YOUNG PEOPLE COMMIT
suicide?

Suicide is a choice made when sadness and depression combine with unclear thinking and the opportunity to commit suicide. It is a decision that is final. Death cannot be turned back into life.

The death of a young person is a terrible tragedy. When a teenager dies, we are painfully aware of all the lost possibilities in his or her life. Suicide is especially tragic because it can often be prevented.

Every case of suicide is different, but common themes can be seen among teenagers who kill themselves. Some suffer from a psychological disorder, such as depression, drug or alcohol abuse, or impulsive, aggressive, and anti-social behavior. Others have family problems, including physical, sexual and emotional abuse, and divorce, or have experienced the death of a loved one. In some cases teens are also suffering from extreme stress in school or in social lives, which may include stress about their sexual identity.

Many people overcome such problems with help and support from friends, family, teachers, and therapists.

But tragically, there are also suicides.

About 2,000 teenagers commit suicide every year in the United States, making it the leading cause of death among people ages ten to twenty-four. Since 1980, the suicide rate among all persons ages ten to nineteen has gone up, especially among African American males. Guns are being used more than ever before, accounting for about two-thirds of all suicides.

Nearly five times more boys than girls commit suicide, but more girls than boys attempt suicide. Some researchers believe the reason more boys are successful in committing suicide is because they are likely to choose violent and irreversible means of killing themselves. But researchers also say that girls tend to be depressed more often than boys. Gay youths are two to three times more likely to attempt suicide than other young people.

It is not our fault when someone makes the horrible choice to take his or her own life. But they can choose to live, if we know how to help.

You can do something to help. In this book, you will learn different ways in which teens have helped each other. You will also learn how *you* can get involved in teen suicide prevention.

❖ HOW CAN TEENS HELP EACH ❖ OTHER COPE WITH PROBLEMS?

1. Learn peer counseling. Teens are more likely to confide in each other than in adults. Learn how to be a better listener through a peer counseling program in your school. Volunteer at your local counseling center.

2. Put yourself "on the lines." Telephone hot-lines are a great way to help. Many programs across the United States train teens to be good listeners and to know what to say when a suicidal person calls for help. You get the satisfaction of helping a stranger, and your counseling skills could come in handy if a friend needs help.

3. Make rounds in a hospital. Teenagers can visit other teens who have been hospitalized after a suicide attempt. Some teen volunteers are survivors of suicide themselves. They learn how to listen, and they understand.

4. Face sexuality. Gay and straight teens can work through community and school-based programs to prevent ignorance about homosexuality and victimization of gay teens.

5. Get on the airwaves. Radio and television can help to spread any message. Teenagers can get involved in school radio and TV stations. With the help of experts, teens can plan programs about suicide awareness and prevention. Teens can even persuade commercial broadcasters to help reach troubled teenagers.

6. Fight suicide in cyberspace. Teens who have learned to be peer counselors may make good online listeners.

7. Fight against substance abuse and fight for gun control. Many suicides are linked to alcohol or drug abuse. Guns are used in suicides more often today than ten years ago. These are two areas of activism directly related to suicide prevention.

❖ QUESTIONS TO ASK YOURSELF ❖

1) What are some reasons for suicide? 2) What is peer counseling? 3) How do peer counselors operate "online"?

If your friend is talking about suicide, take it seriously and tell someone. It may save your friend's life.

chapter

1

PEER COUNSELING

WHAT ARE FRIENDS FOR? A FRIEND IS someone we can have fun with and with whom we can talk about things. One day, a friend may confide in you that he or she is very depressed. What should you do?

Many mental health professionals agree that teens are more likely to talk to each other about problems, rather than go to an adult. That's why it's so important for teens to learn how to respond, and to help.

By becoming peer facilitators in school, teens learn how to react to everyday problems as well as crises, not only for friends but for anyone in school. Nancy Scherlong of Middle Earth Crisis Counseling Center on Long Island trains students to deal with a crisis "peer-to-peer" in local schools.

"Sometimes, I think kids can relate more easily to someone similar to their own background and age when they are upset," says Scherlong.

One of the reasons why people may consider suicide is because they are deeply depressed over the death of a loved one. However, help is available.

Peer facilitators are usually selected by the school staff.

One important skill that students learn is how to recognize serious suicidal actions and statements. They learn that it is important to ask an adult for help, even if it means making your friend angry.

"It's a big stigma, that [people] will be angry if you try to help them," Scherlong says. "But our view is, you would rather have your friends be angry, which is something they will get over, than take their lives, which is permanent."

When someone calls the Middle Earth hotline to ask for advice about a friend, sometimes the outreach center will ask if it's okay to call the friend. A counselor will then call but will talk only to the teen, not to anyone else at home.

"It seems to work pretty well," says Scherlong. "You would think kids would be really angry, but in fact they are just surprised that someone would go to that length to help them."

Teens who are age fifteen and up can volunteer at the Middle Earth Center. "They go with us to health fairs and community events, help us distribute literature, and sometimes do office work to help out," says Scherlong.

❖ HOW TO BEGIN ❖

Suicide prevention really starts with preventing severe depression, says suicide prevention educator David Conroy, who talks to students about how they can help each other. In New York City, like any big city, there are lots of depressed kids.

"There are large numbers of people who have lost a relative through homicide, AIDS, or other illness," Conroy says. "It's a tremendously high-risk situation for depression and suicide."

He tells students that they can be very helpful to younger kids who are grieving. "The main thing in grief work is to let the person talk and let out feelings."

When Conroy was twenty, one of his best friends committed suicide. "It was someone you wouldn't have expected would do this," says Conroy, meaning that his friend seemed happy.

Today, Conroy, forty-nine, uses his friend as an example when he talks to teenagers. His program, called Suicide Prevention Resources, has received government and private funding. He has been working against suicide since he recovered from his own depression years ago. He visits schools and youth programs, and trains counselors who help children and adults. Sometimes, he makes a special visit when a suicide has occurred.

"I make it a point that a low-risk group is not a no-risk group. People in a high-risk group for cancer get it, but people in low-risk groups can get it too."

Conroy tells students about his feelings of guilt over his own friend's death, and how he himself became depressed for several years. "Helping others is a big part of my own recovery," he says.

Conroy knows it can be hard to break the ice when a friend is depressed.

"What happens when someone's mother, friend, or boyfriend dies? We walk on eggshells around them and avoid them, because [we're afraid] we might say the wrong thing."

That's not helpful, he believes. "Kids need a stable friend who is going to be there for them over a long period of time."

But teens should not try to handle a danger-ous situation alone, he warns. He shows stu-dents a newspaper article about a fifteen-year-old girl who committed suicide. "Her friends all knew about [her depression] and tried to help her on their own, but they never told adults," he says. "They should not have kept it a secret."

But there are limits to responsibility. "Suicide happens in much the same way as a heart attack: We don't want it to happen, but it hap-pens. Then some people feel numb, some feel anger."

But in most cases, he adds, "people around the victim were behaving like normal people. Some may not have been aware the person was depressed, or they were afraid they might do the wrong thing. Some people say they did a lot to help but it wasn't enough, or they became exhausted and worn out."

There is no absolute prevention for suicide, Conroy says. "But if we do something instead of nothing, we will have a lot fewer suicides."

❖ SOME SKILLS THAT PEER ❖ COUNSELORS LEARN

It is not always obvious to friends and family that someone is depressed. Depression is a men-tal illness that can be diagnosed by a doctor. Therapy and medications can help the depressed person.

Many teens make the mistake of not telling anyone about a friend's dangerous behavior and are unable to handle the situation themselves.

But if someone never seems happy, and rarely smiles; or if he or she talks a lot about death and ways of dying; or if he or she starts giving away favorite possessions to friends, it is very important to tell an adult. A teacher, guidance counselor, clergyperson, or parent will know how to help.

Clear signs of depression are:

- Feelings of hopelessness, worthlessness, or guilt
- Inability to concentrate, and loss of interest in things that used to give pleasure (sports, reading, talking to friends)
- Trouble sleeping
- Appetite changes—eating too much or too little
- Unexplained aches and pains
- Wanting to be alone, and cutting classes
- Drinking heavily or taking drugs

If a friend confesses to having suicidal feelings, the first thing to do is to listen. Sometimes your friend might say things like, "My parents would be better off without me," or "I'll show my boyfriend how I really feel about our breakup." Or he or she might say, "If I can't go to college, I don't want to live." Stop and listen carefully to what your friend might be trying to tell you. Don't be afraid to ask: "Are you feeling so bad that you really don't want to live?"

Sometimes people are afraid that asking that question might cause a person to think about suicide for the first time. In fact, that's not the case. If your friend has been thinking suicidally, your question may be a huge relief. He or she may be able to talk about it just because you showed that you cared.

❖ SHOULD YOU KEEP A SECRET? ❖

Many times someone who is thinking about suicide confides in a close friend or relative but makes them promise not to tell. We all want to keep our promises, but at times it is better to break a promise. This is one of them. Your friend's life is more important than the principle of keeping a promise.

If you think your friend is in danger, it is important to talk to an adult immediately. It's understandable for you to have conflicting feelings about it. You can tell the adult that, too. The most important thing is that you have made other people aware of the problem. These people can step in to help your friend get through a very difficult time.

❖ QUESTIONS TO ASK YOURSELF ❖

1) Do you confide in friends? 2) Do you think you could be a peer facilitator? 3) How can you help a depressed person? 4) What are some signs of depression?

chapter

2

TELEPHONE HOTLINES

ONE WAY TEENAGERS CAN HELP EACH OTHER is through telephone hotlines.

Michelle, nineteen, decided to go "on the lines" when she was fifteen. She became a volunteer at CONTACT Care Center in Lafayette, California, a telephone hotline. With other volunteers, Michelle learned to listen to callers and to help them help themselves. Recently, her training had a personal benefit when she actually helped a friend who was feeling suicidal. "Just knowing the skills I know helped me a lot," says Michelle. "I didn't feel totally helpless. It would be really scary for anyone to have a friend come to them with a problem and not know what to do."

Teens are more likely to turn to peers than to parents or teachers when they are in trouble, says Joan Emerzian, executive director of CONTACT in Lafayette. Hotline training helps teenagers to reach those troubled friends, she says. They will know what to do.

If you are depressed and need someone to talk to, call a hotline.
Volunteers have been specially trained to help you.

Training lasts about three months at
CONTACT, a branch of the Pennsylvania-based
CONTACT USA organization, which sets up hotlines around the country. Some of the hotlines,
like the one in Lafayette, have teenage volunteers helping anyone who calls. Some of these
callers are teens, but many adults also call to ask
for help with their problems.

The mixed training group is good for everyone, says Emerzian. "Teens learn that adults
have fears and problems and don't know everything, and the adults find out that teenagers do
know things and can even help adults."

Training involves learning skills and sharing

experiences. For Michelle, "It was neat for me to share with older people and other people my age as well, and hear their feedback. I had only shared these things with my sister and my parents, and it made me see how important it is to communicate with other people."

In training, they learned about "concreteness," says Michelle. "That's what really clicked with me. It includes three things: feelings, behavior, and experience. Lots of people are more in tune with their feelings." For instance, if someone is in tears, you don't focus on the fact that he or she is crying. You have to focus on other areas, like what happened and what that person is going to do about it.

"Other people focus more on what happened and what they thought of doing, but there is no emotion in their voices even if they are talking about suicide or something horrible. You have to direct them to see a balance in those categories," says Michelle.

Some common problems are unwanted pregnancies, fear of HIV and AIDS, drug abuse, problems with parents, and relationship issues.

Michelle thinks cultural differences can also be challenging. Teens from immigrant families are "trying to fit in and live up to both their culture and American culture. I have the most difficult time when people say, 'What should I do, my boyfriend bla bla bla.' Those are the hardest, because you have to try to direct them to start thinking about their feelings.

"You have to stop and say, 'I am not here to give advice.' You turn it around and ask, 'What would you do? We are not talking about me. What options have you thought of?' "

Michelle has never had a "high lethality" call. "If someone calls and says, 'I want to kill myself,' the first thing to do—and it may sound insensitive—is ask, 'How do you plan to do it?' If the person's plans are very clear, if he says, 'With pills,' and if you ask 'Where are the pills?' and he says, 'They are in my hand right now,' that is high lethality."

Joan Emerzian says such calls are pretty rare. CONTACT calls 911 or traces a call only if they think someone is really serious. Volunteers are trained to assess the situation: Is there a plan? Is the person giving things away, or writing a suicide note? Does he or she have a gun, and is it loaded?

Says Michelle, "I have had people who have tried to commit suicide before and are thinking of doing it again, but don't have a clear plan. If they are vague about it, you back off and see what is going on: 'What happened to you today that made you feel like this?' "

Like the rest of the volunteers, Michelle helps callers of all ages. Through the training, she realized that she "could relate to adults' problems and they could relate to mine. Even though

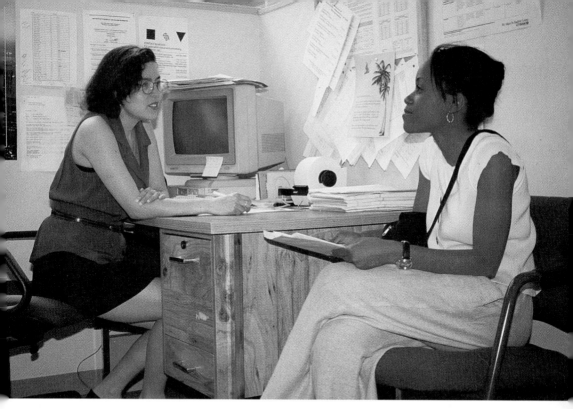

Volunteers for hotlines all receive training before they can work for the hotlines.

their problems are different—about marriage and children and work—their feelings are the same. You can relate to everyone's problems, because we all feel the same way."

Michelle was interested in psychology and why people do the things they do and think the things they think. But it wasn't just an abstract interest for her. One day, a friend told her she was depressed because she didn't think she could meet her parents' expectations.

"She would talk about her frustrations and problems, and it would always come down to the same bottom line," says Michelle. "She was depressed and helpless and didn't want to live any longer."

23

Michelle says she understands and respects her friend. "She had started to question what life is all about and what is important in life. Over the last couple of years she has gotten a better understanding about herself. She realizes that she is a competitive person, but she has a much better idea of what should take priority in relationships. It took a big trauma for her to realize it."

Emerzian says the hotline helps teens make a difference. "If they have problems in their own lives, or friends who have problems, they are not afraid to engage the friends in conversation and encourage them to share their feelings instead of being afraid and walking away or changing the subject." They sometimes encourage a friend to get professional help, even if they think the friend might be mad at them for butting in.

Michelle has encouraged her friends to join the hotline. "These skills have helped me so much," she says. "Communications skills are worth learning."

❖ QUESTIONS TO ASK YOURSELF ❖

1) Have you ever called a telephone hotline? 2) Have you ever wanted to call one? 3) What is "concreteness"? 4) Do you think you could help other teens?

chapter

3

MAKING THE ROUNDS

MANY PEOPLE THINK YOU HAVE TO BE OLDER to be wiser. But teenagers can be wise, too. Sometimes getting through a bad experience makes you strong and wise enough to help someone else do the same.

Take Jessica, for example. She's sixteen, and last year she attempted suicide. "When I was in the hospital psychiatric ward, I decided to help other teens when I got out," she says. "I go to the hospitals near my hometown and talk to teens about my experience."

When a friend started talking about suicide, Jessica asked her therapist what to do or say, without mentioning the friend's name. "It was great, because my friend listened to me, and she did not kill herself," says Jessica.

Another teen, Liz, was hospitalized for a suicide attempt this year, and went through an outpatient treatment program. Afterward, like Jessica, she volunteered to work with other teens in the hospital.

Many teens with suicidal thoughts turn to drugs or alcohol in order to feel good. Marijuana, made from marijuana plants (shown above) is one of the most popular drugs used by teens.

Liz, who had always been interested in psychiatry and psychology, says that she "found it all the more educating being inside the hospital and working with kids. That taught me things I had never come in contact with in my own life."

❖ A SURVIVOR TALKS ❖

"I am a teen. I've been hospitalized, the typical routine. I got involved in a counseling group that is very diverse in age and background. This is where I learned that life is good and I'm good.

"So I love to share my knowledge with others, particularly with teens, because it's such a hard time of life. The decks are stacked against us, and

*furthermore, we're set up against each other. It's
obvious that there are many teens out there hurting
who could really use support.*

*For me, one of the important things about starting
a support group for teens is working on leadership
skills and, of course, making bonds with other teens,
etc."*

❖ PROGRAMS FOR TEENS ❖

Many hospitals have programs in which
teenagers can become involved. Help can
include cheering up patients and sharing your
own experience of recovery from depression.

In College Meadows Hospital in Overland
Park, Kansas, teenagers who have survived a
drug or alcohol overdose can talk to other teens
who are depressed.

"Kids with suicidal thoughts or depression
often turn to drugs or alcohol to feel good,"
says Maggie Jenkins, a chemical dependency
counselor at the hospital. "They need to work
through their problems, instead of acting
impulsively."

Jenkins has "alumni adolescents"—teens who
have been through the hospital and counseling
program and have stayed off drugs and alcohol
at least six months. "They talk to kids who are
in the same situation, kids who have overdosed
or have suicidal ideas."

No special training is given, says Jenkins.

"It's from the gut. They talk about feelings and about hopes and strengths. They talk about their experiences and how they are still struggling and how they get through it."

Many times, the teen counselors give their phone number to the hospitalized teenagers. "When the kids leave the hospital, if things get to where they are not able to cope, they remember the kid they talked to," says Jenkins.

The program also works for the volunteers. Jenkins says, "It keeps them drug-free. When they are helping someone else they are not focusing on their own issues."

Says Jessica, "When I talk to teens, I tell them there is always a better solution than attempting suicide. Go talk to someone. They can help—or talk to me and I can help, depending on the problem."

"After gaining control of my illness, I became an enthusiastic youth counselor who really loves to help," says Liz.

Hospital volunteering in general can help teens become good listeners. "Being around a lot of older people and sick people makes you less afraid of death," says suicide prevention educator David Conroy. "It gives you an understanding of people who are in pain. Then you will be okay if you are with someone who is in pain.

"It's also good to work on a team, because suicide prevention should not be a lone ranger

activity. You want to network with others. You
see that in hospitals, because critically ill people
get a lot of support," says Conroy.

❖ QUESTIONS TO ASK YOURSELF ❖

1) Have you ever visited a psychiatric hospital? 2) Do you think you would need training to
help teens in a hospital? 3) Can you listen well?

chapter

4

FACING SEXUALITY

IT'S TOUGH ENOUGH FOR MOST OF US TO handle teenage sexual awakening, wondering if we are attractive or interesting, figuring out how to make relationships work with the opposite sex.

But when a teenager thinks he or she may be gay, it's even tougher. In many cultures and religions, homosexuality is seen as a sickness or something bad. Homosexuality is not an illness, and most state laws protect homosexual relationships because relationships are a private matter.

But that doesn't make it easier for a gay teenager to feel comfortable with teens who are homophobic—that is, teens who are afraid of homosexuality because they don't understand it. Often, teens tease or even threaten teenagers whom they believe are gay.

Gay youths are two to three times more likely to attempt suicide than other young people, according to a study by Paul Gibson, a therapist in California. Many of the suicides have to do

Gay teens are more likely to commit suicide than other teens because they may be afraid of not fitting in or feel guilty about their sexuality.

with despair over fitting in and feelings of guilt over homosexuality. That's where Pride for Youth can help.

Pride for Youth is a program on Long Island in which gay teenagers who have "come out," or are open about their sexuality, help other teens. It's part of the Middle Earth Crisis Counseling Center, which also has a hotline for teens.

First of all, the volunteers go into schools and talk to high school classes about homophobia and tolerance. They also go to gay and lesbian hang-outs to let teens know that a hotline and counseling are available if they are having problems. The volunteers teach them about safe sex, and provide condoms, which can help prevent the spread of sexually transmitted diseases. Finally, Pride for Youth runs a weekly coffeehouse where gay teens can hang out and talk.

In the schools, the peer educators conduct "a basic homophobia workshop, confronting bias and sexuality issues," says Pierce Mills, health education specialist for Pride for Youth. "The teens talk about how they deal with it, so the class can no longer say that they have never met anyone who is gay.

"Hopefully, the students develop an inner sensitivity, so if they have a friend who 'comes out' to them, they will be more supportive and refer that friend to services so that he or she will not feel so alone and isolated."

The peer educators also talk about AIDS prevention. They also discuss other issues that gay teens often face, including depression, substance abuse, running away, or being thrown out of their homes.

"All the issues are interrelated," says Mills. "We talk about basic self-esteem issues for gay teens, and how they relate to the self-esteem issues of anyone. We try to show how important it is to be sensitive. Everyone has problems."

The program helps teens to be more sensitive to their friends. It also lets gay teens know— without singling them out—that there is a place where they can get advice and help from other understanding people.

Most volunteers are in their late teens or early twenties. They have to be old enough to have some distance from their own issues, says Mills.

While there are other hotlines for teens on Long Island, there is only one coffeehouse. They don't serve alcohol, but they sometimes show movies.

"A lot of gay teens don't have anywhere to go," says Mills. "The coffeehouse provides a safe alternative to gay bars. They may not be ready for mixing with alcohol and adults."

❖ QUESTIONS TO ASK YOURSELF ❖

1) Do you know anybody who is gay? 2) How does the person feel about his or her sexuality? 3) Do you think you could help a teen who is facing the possibility of being homosexual?

chapter

5

GET ON THE AIRWAVES

THE AIRWAVES ARE A GREAT WAY TO GET ALL kinds of messages across. Teenagers can get involved in school radio and TV stations. They can even influence commercial broadcasters to help reach out to troubled teenagers.

Young radio host Louisa Chu of Chicago says it was not so difficult to set up a program on teen suicide prevention. She had the help of many volunteers and professionals, and that made a difference.

The program started as a way to remember grunge rock artist Kurt Cobain of the music group Nirvana, who killed himself with a shotgun in April 1994. Fans were terribly upset when it happened. Mental health professionals feared that some teens might think suicide was cool if their favorite rock musician did it.

On the first anniversary of Cobain's death, Chu, then a twenty-eight-year-old host on a Chicago alternative rock radio station Q-101,

The death of musician Kurt Cobain raised many people's awareness about suicide.

organized a five-hour call-in show "specifically for teen suicide prevention." The evening program included conversations with teenagers who had tried to kill themselves, with parents and friends of people who had committed suicide, and with teen-suicide prevention experts.

A teacher and some students from a high school support group talked about their problems and how they dealt with them. "It was really powerful," says Chu. "We also had at least two kids who had attempted suicide and were working through their problems. It was powerful to hear from kids in the process of recovery. And we had a group of people who had lost loved ones to suicide."

Chu had two professional counselors on standby from CONTACT Chicago, the local hotline, in case callers wanted help off the air. "They were on the phone straight, for five to six hours," she says.

"I don't think there is a teen today who is not working with some kind of stress or anxiety," says Debra Berger, executive director of CONTACT Chicago, "whether it's with school or family, making decisions, or getting school projects in. They seem to be under a lot more stress than I remember."

Louisa Chu says she was shocked to hear how stressed out some kids were feeling. "It was really sobering and frightening to hear the depth of

Some radio stations have programs in which teens can call in to talk about their problems.

emotion coming from kids as young as eleven." But she was also happy to learn that the radio program seemed to have helped a lot of people. Many teens called the station after the show.

"One teenager didn't sound too emotional, but he asked for the number of the suicide prevention program we had been talking about," says Chu. "I gave him the information and asked him, 'How are you doing?' And he said, 'Things are real bad.' "

Chu talked to him for a short while, but she knew she did not have the right skills to help. "I told him he really needed to talk to people at

CONTACT Chicago because they would help him immediately. He said he would call them right away.

"A week later, he called to thank me. He was getting some help."

In Syracuse, New York, a pop radio station runs a weekly program called Teen Talk, a call-in forum. Teenagers volunteer to be on-air hosts and to screen incoming calls, and professional counselors talk to teens off or on the air. Around 10,000 teens listen in each week, says John Cook, mental health director of CONTACT Syracuse.

Teen volunteers go through an audition and training program. About fifteen volunteers are on duty at any given time, says Cook, who is glad to advise teens who want to start such programs in their own hometowns.

❖ QUESTIONS TO ASK YOURSELF ❖

1) Did you ever call a call-in show? 2) Were you nervous? 3) Would it be easier to be on the other side, hosting the show and taking the calls?

chapter

6

FIGHTING SUICIDE IN CYBERSPACE

THERE ARE GREAT POSSIBILITIES FOR communication through online computer services, as millions of people sign on to them. Suicide is one of the thousands of topics you can talk about online. Help can be found there.

Sometimes teens who have overcome depression or survived suicide attempts leave messages on computer bulletin boards offering to be listeners to other teens. They may not have professional training, but they sometimes have a lot of common sense.

The following are examples of some messages left on computer bulletin boards:

"I have just about every problem you can imagine on my shoulders. My parents won't let me live my life, I have started to go to parties with my friends where everyone gets drunk and/or stoned. I am failing school because I have a learning disability, and the school refuses to help me with it. The

only good thing in my life is my boyfriend, which isn't really a good thing anymore 'cause we had sex for the first time for both of us last week and now I am having major regrets. And it also seems like no one knows what I am going through."

"Hi. I can't believe you would actually go through all those messages just to read this one, but thanks for doing it. I am depressed. It's nothing serious; everybody feels this way once in a while. So if you want to talk, e-mail me."

"My name is Anita, and I really enjoy helping people understand and cope with their problems. I have had a share of my own and can offer advice on just about anything. I am a junior in high school, and I am working toward my career goal of psychiatry. If you need anyone to talk to, leave a message. I will be glad to help."

"I, too, am available for anyone who needs me. I am an active member in a peer counseling group and have gone through proper training. I also go to a teen support group and see people for my own problems. I deal personally with depression, death of a loved one, suicidal related topics, drug abuse, alcoholism of family members, and the list goes on. I am also trained to deal with eating disorders, divorce, dysfunctional families, drug/alcohol abuse, etc. Seek us out if you need someone to talk to."

Many teens go online to talk about or share their problems with others.

"I would like everyone who feels they are alone and that life is a living hell, to please e-mail me! I know what it feels like to suffer from anger, sadness, frustration, and confusion. I have been fighting depression for five years now and I think I may be able to help. I have been raped, sexually abused, and sexually harassed. I plan to start school in the fall to become a psychology major. My dream is to help people, no matter what you are going through or have gone through."

Most professionals say you should not try to advise others on serious matters, aside from listening and maybe sharing what you have learned. Before offering to be a listener online, it's a good idea to talk to people from a hotline organization. Find out if they can give you some training in how to be a good listener, how to recognize danger signs, and what kinds of questions to ask and what to avoid.

David Conroy believes that electronic mail can be helpful for some. "It's a way not to be completely lonely, but it doesn't have anywhere near the effect of a face-to-face contact. E-mail does not break down the isolation and loneliness."

❖ A SURVIVOR TALKS ❖

"When I was fifteen, I was hospitalized for a year and a half for suicide. I had been suicidal for at

*least three years. I believe that if someone had been
there who recognized the signs (and there were lots of
signs) and knew what to do, I would not have needed to be hospitalized. I know a lot about the signs
because I probably gave off every one except for
admitting myself to a hospital.*

*"Almost everyone but my parents knew. Adults
really don't understand a lot of times, and they deny
that their kids could have problems. All my friends
knew, and all they did was say, 'Promise you won't
do that again,' or 'Stop that.' They never really
helped me.*

*"To people who are depressed, I would say hang
in there, try to get help. Take it one day at a time,
and keep a feelings log (journal) to get your feelings
out. Just let it all out of your system.*

*"I am very open about my problems. I try to let
other people know they are not alone and it has and
is happening to others.*

*"I figure since I know through experience how
people felt, I could help, especially since I recovered.
Right now, I just participate in online groups and e-
mail individuals with problems.*

*"The best way to help someone is to make things
available to them and make sure they are confiden-
tial. The other important thing is making it clear
that they won't be arrested or put away. Kids are
scared that if people find out they have problems
they will be locked up. There are other ways, including day programs, private therapy, group therapy,*

family therapy, and outpatient medications with a psychiatrist."

❖ **QUESTIONS TO ASK YOURSELF** ❖

1) Do you have a computer at home or school? 2) Have you ever communicated online? 3) Would you like to help other teens online? 4) What should you do to prepare yourself?

chapter

7

TAKING ACTION

❖ AGAINST SUBSTANCE ABUSE ❖

Two other areas of activism are directly related to suicide prevention: drug and alcohol abuse and gun control. Many suicides have been linked to alcohol or drug abuse. Guns are more easily available and are used in suicides more often today than ten years ago.

Some professionals believe that one way to prevent suicides is to limit access to alcohol, since a person who is drinking is more likely to act impulsively. Many teens may not be aware of how alcohol can affect them. One of the effects of alcohol is that it tends to make users lose their inhibitions. A teen who is depressed may not think seriously about taking his or her own life when sober, but alcohol or drug use can cloud a user's judgment. The influence of drugs or alcohol can make a person express anger or depression through suicidal behavior.

According to Students Against Driving

SADD was formed by a group of teens to help other teens stop drinking and driving. If drinking and driving is a problem in your community, speak with your friends about how you can help end the problem.

Drunk, or SADD, car crashes are the number one killer of young people today. Roughly half of all teen crashes are alcohol- or drug-related. Every three hours, a teen is killed in this kind of crash.

SADD was formed in 1981 by a group of teens in an effort to help other teens stop drinking and driving and to spread the message about the dangers of alcohol and drugs. To find out how to start a local chapter, or for information about the dangers of drinking call their headquarters in Marlboro, Massachusetts at (508) 481-3568.

❖ **FOR GUN CONTROL** ❖
Another suggestion is to have strict gun con-

trol laws. One reason why guns are used more often in suicides today may be because they are more easily available.

Teens and guns often make a deadly combination. Some people believe that if guns were not so accessible, the chances of teens using them to commit suicide would decrease. Others argue that even if guns aren't available, people will find ways to kill themselves. But other methods commonly used in suicide attempts, such as overdosing on pills, sometimes fail, while injuries that result from gun wounds are more often fatal. More than 50 percent of people age twenty-five or younger who kill themselves do so with a gun. In 1990, handguns were used in 12,000 suicides.

Handgun Control, Inc., in Washington, DC, tries to educate people about the dangers of handguns. They have a fact sheet on "Firearms and Youth Suicide," and their education department works with schools to teach about gun safety. Call them at (202) 898-0792 for more information.

❖ QUESTIONS TO ASK YOURSELF ❖

1) Does your town have a chapter of SADD? 2) Do you think you or your friends would be interested in starting one? 3) Do you have any ideas about reducing the number of guns among teenagers?

chapter

8

WHAT IF IT HAS ALREADY HAPPENED?

IT IS NATURAL TO FEEL SORROW, ANGER, guilt, and helplessness after the death of someone you love. It's important to understand that you are not responsible for the person's death, even if you had an idea that he or she might have been depressed.

It is most important to talk about your feelings with a parent, counselor, teacher, or therapist. It is also important to learn to recognize signs of severe depression, both in yourself and others, and to take these signs seriously.

Paul was sixteen when his stepfather died of cancer. They had been close friends, and Paul was very upset. He missed his stepdad a lot, and he knew his mom was having trouble paying the huge medical bills.

When Paul got a speeding ticket, he became even more depressed. He became worried about how his mom would pay for everything. He felt that no one could be proud of him, because he

You may feel grief, anger, and guilt over the death of someone you love, but you are not responsible for that person's death.

thought the ticket meant he had failed at something.

A friend's dad offered to lend him money to pay for the ticket. Paul accepted. Later that day, he told his mom he was going out. He never came back. Instead, he went to a river, jumped off a bridge and drowned.

❖ A FINAL WAY OUT ❖

To us it might seem that Paul's problems could have been solved another way. He had good friends who wanted to help. But Paul was depressed, and depression is a kind of illness that can block clear thinking. Instead of seeing his problems as temporary hurdles to overcome, Paul saw them as a wall over which he could not climb. Instead of having hope and thinking about the future and all its possibilities, he only thought about his failures. He thought his friends would love him more after he died. Instead of realizing that his mother would be horrified, Paul thought she would be better off without him.

For Paul, lots of difficult problems piled up in a very short time. He had real reasons to be sad. He may have felt unable to take control of his life, because every time he turned around he was hit by another blow. By taking his life, he took ultimate control—for the last time.

Very few people make the terrible decision Paul made. One other person who did, and survived, said, "From the instant I saw my hand leave the railing, I knew I wanted to live. I was terrified out of my skull!"

❖ GETTING HELP ❖

It's important to know that it's okay to feel sad, angry, or low sometimes. But it is not normal to always be depressed. If you know someone who feels that way, don't wait another minute: Talk to an adult you trust.

After Paul's death, psychologists talked to students in his school. Through seminars and counseling sessions, they helped the students to cope.

A suicide often brings about changes in a community's thinking as well as in education that can prevent other tragedies.

Help was available for them. For Paul, it was too late. Sometimes, a suicide brings on a change in thinking that can prevent other tragedies.

In the late 1980s, the teenage members of a religious youth organization chapter excluded one girl. The girl later committed suicide, and the others felt guilty. The organization then sponsored a suicide-prevention program in its chapters, says Charlotte Ross. Ross founded the Suicide Prevention and Crisis Center in Burlingame, California. It has a twenty-four-hour crisis hotline that is used by teenagers and also by counselors in need of advice.

In another case, a boy killed himself on the

second day of school after his family had moved to California from the Midwest. "He was so alone and so afraid, it seemed overwhelming," says Ross. "It was heartbreaking."

In response, the students created a 'befriender program' for one-to-one contact with any transfer students and new freshmen. It prepares them to be future good neighbors.

Some professionals think it's a bad idea to have teens too involved in suicide prevention, because they are worried about teens romanticizing the subject.

But Ross disagrees. "We don't actually believe it is controversial to involve adolescents in suicide prevention. Kids do romanticize suicide, and that's why prevention is needed: to let them know it's not romantic and to let them know it is safe for kids to talk about their feelings and concerns. Kids do turn to kids, and we should be able to make kids better helpers."

❖ QUESTIONS TO ASK YOURSELF ❖

1) What can you do if someone close to you commits suicide? 2) Should friends feel guilty? 3) How can you help prevent suicide among teens?

chapter

9

WHAT'S AVAILABLE IN YOUR COMMUNITY

IN CALIFORNIA, PUBLIC HIGH SCHOOLS HAVE a special suicide-prevention curriculum. It's a four- or five-hour program, spread out over a few weeks. All students get homework assignments to find out what they would do or where they could go for help if a friend were feeling suicidal. By the last session, they must report on what is available locally, and what isn't.

"Some kids come back and report that the majority of resources in the community require parental consent, or have fees that kids can't pay, or have a waiting list," says Charlotte Ross of the Suicide Prevention and Crisis Center.

She believes the program "helps teenagers to have a role in helping their community develop appropriate resources." And it helps in the healing process that many kids need. If they have lost someone or have grief, they need to be able to do something. Suicidal behavior leaves you

Incorporating suicide prevention classes into a school's curriculum helps teens in the healing process.

frustrated: You wonder what should or could have been done. Working against it can be very healthy because it helps you to heal.

Teens can often feel overwhelmed by the problems that they face in school, home, or problems arising from their changing bodies. They may not know how to deal with these problems and can become depressed. Or if a friend suddenly confesses that he or she has been thinking about "ending it all," a teen may not know how to help.

That's why it can be useful for teens to be aware of what help is available to them. Your local community is one of the best places to go

for help if you or a friend are depressed and need someone to talk to.

❖ QUESTIONS TO ASK YOURSELF ❖

1) Does your school have a suicide-prevention program? 2) Do you know of any resources in your community for depressed teenagers? 3) How might you get involved helping other teens?

GLOSSARY

chemical dependency A physical addiction to a drug or other chemical.

cyberspace Computer system that uses interactive hardware and software.

depression Mental disorder marked by feelings of sadness and hopelessness, as well as difficulty in thinking or concentrating.

facilitator Person who assists the progress of another person or group of persons in an undertaking.

feedback Reaction or response to a statement or an activity.

homophobia Fear and/or hatred of homosexuals.

homosexuality Sexual preference for members of one's own sex.

hotline Telephone connection that provides access to counseling or professional service.

instability Lack of emotional or physical steadiness.

irreversible Incapable of being undone or changed.

psychiatric ward Area of a hospital devoted to care of the mentally ill.

stress Physical response to a circumstance, such as fear or pain, that interferes with normal behavior.

survivor One who lives through a life-threatening situation.

Organizations to Contact

WHETHER YOU WANT TO VOLUNTEER OR GET advice for yourself or a friend, the following sources may be helpful.

HOSPITAL VOLUNTEERING
Call your local hospital's community relations department or psychiatric division. Ask if they or any other nearby hospital uses teenage volunteers to help kids who are hospitalized for depression. If they say you need training, ask where you can get the training.

If there is no program, don't give up. If necessary, you can try to start one by getting in touch with the psychiatric division. You can use the chapter on hospital volunteering in this book as an example of what you might want to do.

❖ PEER COUNSELING ❖
To find a suicide-prevention hotline and peer counseling program in your area, call The American Association of Suicidology, Washington, DC; (202) 237-2280. Ask for the

current number or address of a few suicide-
prevention and crisis intervention agencies in
your area.

CONTACT USA
Pouch A
Harrisburg, PA 17105-1300
(717) 232-3501
Ask if there is a teen-to-teen counseling program
near you. CONTACT will help students set up
local programs.

**National Depressive and Manic-Depressive
Association**
730 North Franklin Street
Chicago, IL 60610
(312) 642-7243, or toll free (800) 826-3632
Ask for the chapter closest to you and for their
list of publications on depression.

PEER COUNSELING FOR GAY YOUTH:
Call Pride for Youth at (516) 679-9000.

**For information on recognizing depression
and what to do if a friend is suicidal:**

**National Institute on Mental Health,
Department of Health and Human
Services**
Public Inquiries, Room 15-C-05

5600 Fishers Lane
Rockville, MD 20857
Ask for the following pamphlets:
"Depression/Awareness, Recognition, Treatment;
  a guide for students from NIMH"
"What to Do When a Friend Is Depressed"
"Depression: Effective Treatments Are Available"
(301) 443–4513
e-mail: nimhinfo@nih.gov

Youth Suicide National Center
West Coast Office
1811 Trousdale Drive
Burlingame, CA 94010
(415) 573-3950
Ask for pamphlet "Suicide in Youth and What
  You Can Do About It."

RADIO AND TV

For advice on getting a program on the air,
talk to the producer of Teen Talk at CONTACT
Syracuse: (315) 425-5318.

If your school has a closed-circuit radio or TV
program, tell the faculty adviser what you would
like to do. But before you talk about it, be prepared with the names of local or national suicide
prevention organizations you plan to call.

Offer a concept, but be flexible. For example,
you may not be able to do a five-hour program
like the one in Chicago. But one or two hours

of conversation and music might be enough to let other students know more about suicide and where they can volunteer or seek help themselves.

Some people want to share their personal experiences with others without using their names. Be prepared to accept those conditions, as long as it is someone you and your adviser have met and trust.

If your school has no broadcast program, contact your favorite radio station. Tell them what you have in mind, and tell them about the successful program in Chicago. Offer to get involved, as much as your schoolwork will allow.

FOR FURTHER READING

Gootman, Marilyn E. *When a Friend Dies: A Book for Teens About Grieving and Healing.* Minneapolis, Minnesota: Free Spirit, 1995.

Kuklin, Susan. *After a Suicide: Young People Speak Up.* New York: Putnam, 1995.

Nelson, Richard E., and Galas, Judith C. *The Power to Prevent Suicide.* Minneapolis, Minnesota: Free Spirit, 1995.

Schleifer, Jay. *Everything You Need to Know About Teen Suicide.* Rev. ed. New York: Rosen Publishing Group, 1993.

Smith, Judie. *Drugs and Suicide.* Rev. ed. New York: Rosen Publishing Group, 1993.

INDEX

ABOUT THE AUTHOR

Toby Axelrod is an award-winning journalist living in New York City. She writes for *The Jewish Week* and has a column in *The New York Observer*.

PHOTO CREDITS: Cover photo © A/P Wide World; pp. 2, 16 by Michael Brandt; p. 10 © Image Bank/Maria Taglienti; p. 12 by Lauren Piperno; p. 23 by Maria Moreno; p. 20 by Lauren Piperno; p. 26 by Katie McClancy; p. 31 by Kyle Wagner; p. 35 © A/P Wide World; p. 37 by Yung-Hee Chia; p. 41 by Matthew Baumann/Kim Sonsky; p. 46 by Kim Sonsky; p. 49 © Impact Visuals/C. Takagi; p. 51 © Impact Visuals/Evan Johnson; p. 54 © Impact Visuals/Loren Santow.

PHOTO RESEARCH: Vera Amadzadeh

DESIGN: Kim Sonsky